HIST DOCUMENTS AND PHOTOGRAPHS OF TOMBSTONE

by Ben T. Traywick

Published by
Red Marie's Bookstore
P.O. Box 891
Tombstone, Arizona 85638

Printing and Design by
WE PRINT IT, INC.
—Los Angeles—

Historical Documents and Photographs of Tombstone

To a lady called Red Marie

© Copyright 1971 by Ben T. Traywick
© Copyright 1994 by Ben T. Traywick

All rights reserved.
No portion of this book may be copied or reprinted without permission of the copyright owner.

Published by
Red Marie's Bookstore

First Printing: 1971

Revised Edition: 1994

Printing and Design by
WE PRINT IT, INC.
—Los Angeles—

TABLE OF CONTENTS

Author's Foreword ii

Section 1: Historical Photographs 1

Section 2: Historical Documents 121

AUTHOR'S FOREWORD

When I moved to Tombstone in 1968, much of the local history was still readily available. Legal documents were still in place in the Tombstone City Hall, the County Courthouse in Bisbee, and in the Historical Society as well as in some of the private homes.

In a very short while, I began to notice that the original documents and photographs were rapidly disappearing. Collectors were beginning to pay large amounts of cash with no questions asked, for these historical items.

Although these items were the property of the citizens, unscrupulous officials, writers, and collectors were removing these pieces of history for their own use. I realized that I could not stem the tide of theft, but that there was a way in which I could ensure a record would be left for the future generations.

I immediately began a program of copying every item of Tombstone history that I deemed important. It was expensive, but satisfying in that, in many cases, my copies are now the only record left. During the past quarter century, my archives have expanded to thousands of documents and photographs, and have become one of the best such collections anywhere.

Friends and complete strangers alike have been instrumental in helping me build this collection. Many, many individuals have come by my office for some historical conversation and then mailed me priceless information.

A few years back, a lawyer from Tennessee came in to inquire about his great grandfather, who had owned Ritchie's Dance Hall. When he had returned home, he sent me thirteen C.S. Fly photographs, seven of which I had never seen.

Just this year, a man who owns a tattoo parlor in Memphis, supplied me a missing link in the Clanton family. A lady from Missouri has been sending me information on that same family for a number of years. They are interested relatives.

The interest and the efforts of these historically inclined people, plus that of the descendants of Tombstone's pioneers, and my own research, has provided the sources from which the contents of this book come.

Ben T. Traywick

Historical Photographs

Historical Documents and Photographs of Tombstone

Lucky Cuss Mine

Historical Photographs

Tombstone 1882.

Small Mine Miners.

Gird's Mill.

Shaft House of the Toughnut Mine.

Historical Photographs

Sixteen-horse team hauling Tombstone Ore.

Pittsburgh-Arizona Mining Company Mill.

Sulphuret Mine Head Frame.

Historical Photographs

Luck Sure Mine

Four boilers weighing 25 tons each with a combined capacity of over 1,000 H.P. at the Tombstone Consolidated Mine.

Historical Documents and Photographs of Tombstone

North Bonanza Shaft

A mule train files from the "diggings" of a mine near Tombstone in this photograph taken in the early 1900's.

—Epitaph Photo.

Historical Photographs

Glory Hole, corner Fifth & Toughnut.

A snap shot below the water level.

Shaft House of the West Side Mine.

Hoisting works, Lucky Cuss Mine.

--Historical Society

Historical Photographs

Grand Central Hoisting Works and Mine Office.

Giant Cornish pumps kept water out of the mines for a while.

Historical Documents and Photographs of Tombstone

Ed Schieffelin, dressed for a prospecting trip in the hills about Tombstone, with Bowie knife, gun, canteen, and pick.

Historical Photographs

Brunckow's bloody cabin.

Richard Gird
Was a partner of the Schieffelin brothers.

Richard Gird, Al and Ed Schieffelin 1880.

Knights of Pythias, 1885, on Fremont Street.

Ed Schieffelin,
who discovered a mountain of silver.

George Whitwell Parsons
kept a factual Diary while in Tombstone.

Historical Photographs

Edward Lawrence Schieffelin founded Tombstone.

Wyatt Berry Stapp Earp, 1881.
—*Glenn Boyer collection*

Historical Photographs

Wyatt Earp in his 20's.
—Glenn Boyer collection

Wyatt Earp and Bat Masterson.

Wyatt Earp
—Glenn Boyer collection

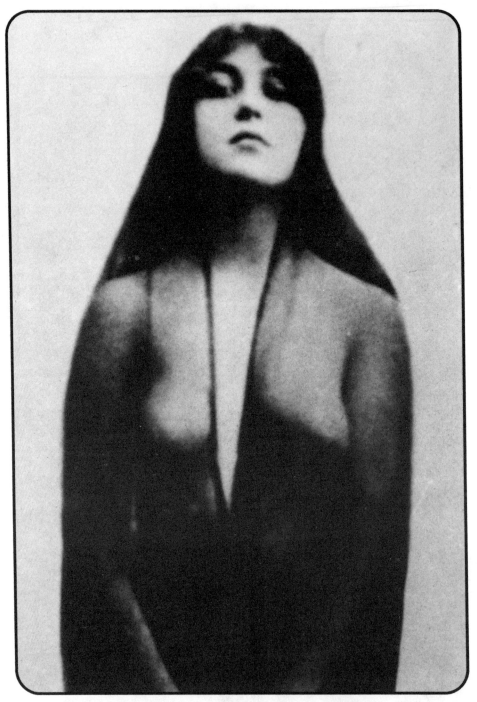

Josephine Marcus Earp, Wyatt's third wife.
—Glenn Boyer collection

Wyatt Earp's last portrait photo before his final illness.
—Glenn Boyer collection

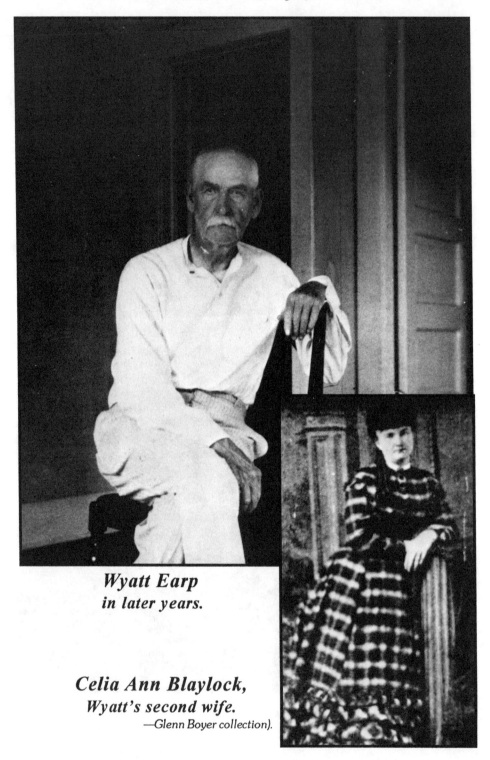

Wyatt Earp
in later years.

Celia Ann Blaylock,
Wyatt's second wife.
—Glenn Boyer collection).

Historical Photographs

Morgan S. Earp
—*Glenn Boyer collection.*

Morgan's wife, Louisa Earp.
—*Glenn Boyer collection*

Virgil Walter Earp
—*Courtesy Hildreth Halliwell*

Virgil's wife, Allie.
—*Courtesy Hildreth Halliwell*

Historical Photographs

Warren Earp at 20.
—Glenn Boyer collection

Warren Baxter Earp
—Glenn Boyer collection

Virgil Earp and two of his nieces.
—Courtesy of Hildreth Halliwell

James Cooksey Earp

Alvira Sullivan Earp, Virgil's wife
—Glenn Boyer collection

Historical Photographs

Gunfight at the O.K. Corral recreated at the same time, same place, same way as the original - 100 years later by Tombstone's famous Wild Bunch - October 26, 1981.

Nellie Cashman, Angel of the camp.

Dr. George Emery Goodfellow
"*the Gunfighter's Surgeon.*"

*Charlie Wentworth
one-time Mayor
of Tombstone.*

*"Honest" John
Montgomery,
Co-owner O.K. Corral.*

*William Greene
also known as
"The Copper King."*

Historical Photographs

John Henry "Doc" Holliday.

"Big Nose" Kate,
girlfriend of
"Doc" Holliday
—Glenn Boyer collection

Thomas Clark McLaury
Younger of the McLaury brothers who died in the Gunfight at the O.K. Corral.

Will R. McLaury
Tried to hang the Earps and Holliday for the deaths of his brothers.

Robert Findley McLaury
Older of the two brothers who died in the Gunfight at the O.K. Corral.

Newman Haynes
"Old Man" Clanton.

Joseph Isaac Clanton.

Eddie Foy performance in Schieffelin Hall, Tombstone, Arizona, 1883.

Tombstone Prospector
-C.S. Fly Photo

Historical Photographs

John Swain Slaughter *came to Tombstone with John Slaughter.*

Burt Alvord *A lawman turned outlaw.*

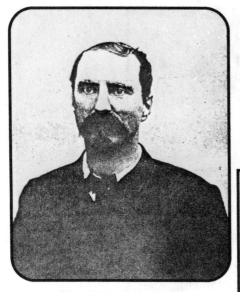

Charlie Thomas
*Mayor of Tombstone about 1881.
Died Bisbee June 30, 1923*

Ely's Photographic Gallery,

312 Fremont Street,

TOMBSTONE, A. T.

Copies may be had at any time.

Marcus A. Smith
Tombstone Lawyer

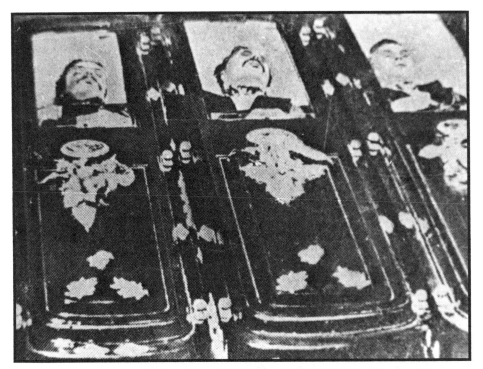

Losers in the Gunfight at the O.K. Corral.

Cosmopolitan Hotel - Tombstone, Arizona, 1882.
A. Billike, Proprietor

Tombstone Court House, 1882.

Left to right, standing: Bill Bradley, Deputy Sheriff; George W. Swain, County Attorney; (Name unknown), Clerk; A. H. Emanuel, Clerk of Court; (Name unknown); William Ritchie, Jailer; Nat Hawke. Seated, center: D. K. Wardell; Mrs. Bluette. Seated, lower row: W. E. Steahle, Attorney; M. D. Scribner, County Treasurer; H. W. Wentworth, County Recorder; W. D. Monmonier.

Historical Photographs

*John P. Clum,
Mayor*
**Postmaster of
Tombstone
Editor of the
Epitaph**

*Mary Dennison
Ware Clum*
**Mrs. John Clum died
in Tombstone and is
buried in
Boothill.**

Historical Documents and Photographs of Tombstone

"Buckskin Frank" Leslie
A notorious ladies' man and, secretly, a Wells-Fargo informer.

Peter Spencer
Outlaw and killer.

Dick Clark
Tombstone gambler. His widow married Billy King.

Henry C. Hooker
Friend of the Earps.

Colonel and Judge William Herring
Friend of the Earps.

Historical Documents and Photographs of Tombstone

Milt Joyce
Owner of the Oriental
—courtesy Harry Stewart

Johnny Speck (pictured here with his Son) At one time, owned the Crystal Palace.

Historical Photographs

James Duncan
Justice of the Peace, Tombstone.
—C.S. Fly Photo

Howard Herring
July 18, 1885.
—from a C.S. Fly Photo

James Potter
Came to Tombstone in 1881 with the third herd of cattle John Slaughter brought from Texas.
—from a C.S. Fly Photo

Historical Photographs

Tombstone Baseball Team and Manager 1887.

—from a C.S. Fly Photo

Three unidentified persons.

At right: Dr. and Mrs. Willis, their children and houseboy. His doctor's office, in the background, was located on the southwest corner of Fremont and 6th Streets at 552 Fremont. Willis was killed in the O.K. Corral on January 3, 1891, by Ben Shanklin, guard at the "Old Guard" Mine.

Historical Documents and Photographs of Tombstone

Jefferson Davis Milton
Texas Ranger, Deputy Sheriff, Stock Association Detective
Wells Fargo Special Agent, U.S. Customs Border Patrolman
Deputy U.S. Marshall, El Paso Police Chief, Chinese Agent for
U.S., Immigration Agent.

Historical Photographs

A. H. Emanuel
One time Mayor of Tombstone.
—from a printed reproduction of a photo in the Brophy collection

Deputy Marshall Kiv Phillips
He was killed in the line of duty by Filomeno Orante in the Moses and Wheeler Saloon on July 8, 1882

Historical Photographs

John Horton Slaughter
—C.S. Fly Photo

Cora Viola Howell
married John Slaughter

Mr. and Mrs. Amazon Howell.
—from a C.S. Fly Photo

Mrs. Amazon (Mary Ann) Howell
John Slaughter's Mother-in-law.
—from a C.S. Fly Photo

Amazon Howell, 1880's
John Slaughter's Father-in-law.
—*from a C.S. Fly Photo*

Historical Documents and Photographs of Tombstone

Wake Benge, Tal Roland, Jeff Lewis
Worked as cowboys for John H. Slaughter, July 1879.
All came to Arizona with Mr. Slaughter's first herd.
The first two went back for the second herd.

Nellie Cashman
As she appeared on July 4, 1886

Historical Documents and Photographs of Tombstone

Camillus Sidney Fly
Tombstone's famous photographer.

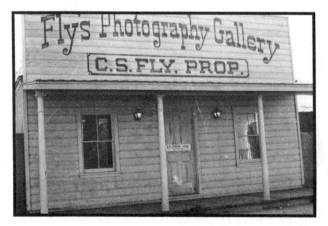

Fly's Photography Gallery
A present day photograph, showing the shop as it is now restored.

Molly E. Fly
Wife of C.S. Fly.

John Harris Behan
First Sheriff of Cochise County.

John Dunbar
(shown here with his Son)
He owned the Dexter Stable with John Behan.

Historical Photographs

William Breakenridge
His claim to fame wouldn't stand up.

Wells Spicer
Justice in O.K. Corral Inquest.

Historical Documents and Photographs of Tombstone

Tombstone's first Fire Department, 1881.
—C.S. Fly Photo

Hose Team Number One
Tombstone's Volunteer Fire Department, 1883
—C.S. Fly Photo

Oriental Saloon.

Fatty Ryan
Saloon owner and one time Chief of Police in Tombstone.

John Peters Ringo
Was never in a real gunfight.

Historical Photographs

Ringo's grave in The Chiricahuas.

Historical Documents and Photographs of Tombstone

William Ritchie and W.R. Johnson.

Ritchie owned Ritchie's Dance Hall.
—courtesy Wm. Stanifer

Jennie Keir Ritchie
Wife of William Ritchie and Viola Cora Slaughter Ritchie shown on the front porch at John Slaughter's ranch.
—courtesy Wm. Stanifer

Historical Photographs

Allen English
Tombstone lawyer.
—from a C.S. Fly Photo

Fly's Photographic Gallery,

312 Fremont Street,

TOMBSTONE, A. T.

Copies may be had at any time.

Mr. Sharkey
He installed the first Tombstone Telephone.

Historical Documents and Photographs of Tombstone

Interior view of W.R. King's modern blacksmith establishment on NW corner of Allen and Third streets.

A. Wentworth

Oldtime County Treasurer of Cochise County. He is pictured here in his flowing white hair that resulted from a political vow. Wentworth was so chagrined when William Jennings Bryan was defeated for the Presidency that he swore he would let his hair grow until another Democrat was in the White House. The mayor of Tombstone at the time this photo was made, Wentworth also was at one time the proprietor of a saloon formerly located at about the present location of the Lucky Cuss Restaurant.

-Photo courtesy of Fred Bennett.

Historical Photographs

Fred Dodge
Undercover man for Wells Fargo.

Bob Paul,
Sheriff Pima County.

Historical Documents and Photographs of Tombstone

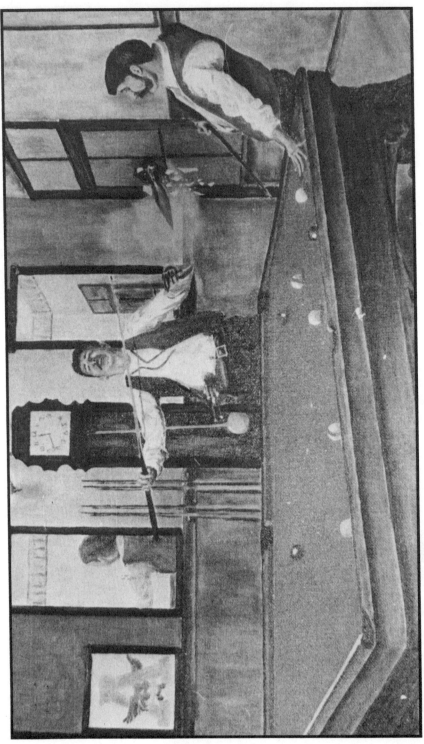

— from a painting by T. Russell

The Killing of Morgan Earp

Luke Short

James Howell, Stonewall Howell & Jesse Fisher.
—*from a C.S. Fly photo*

Historical Photographs

Joe Bignon
Owner of the Bird Cage Theatre.

Big Minnie Bignon
*Wife of Joe Bignon,
who billed her as
230 lbs. of loveliness in pink tights.*

Historical Photographs

LIZETTE THE FLYING NYMPH
came to Tombstone as an actress with the Monarch Carnival Company. She saw the potential for a comely lass such as she in the boom town and stayed on to eventually become a Madam.

The Great White Way
(that was), Sixth and Allen - a portion of Tombstone's Red Light District.

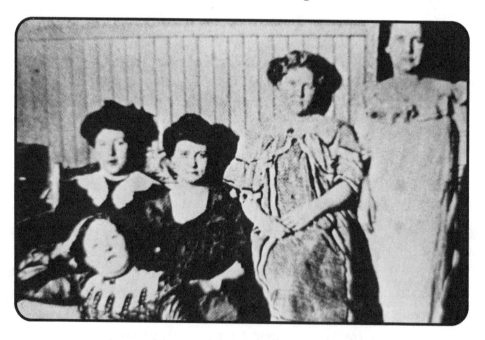

Some of the girls on Sixth Street.

Blonde Mollie
*A Red Light Girl
Eventually she was killed
by Frank Leslie.*

Blonde Marie
A French Madam.

Historical Photographs

May Davenport
A Madam who moved to Cananea, Mexico when the mines in Tombstone flooded.

Crazy Horse Lil
When drunk she would fight man, woman or beast.

Birdic Woods
The fallen angel that May Killeen claimed Buckskin Frank committed adultery with when she filed for divorce from the famous gunman. Leslie did not contest the divorce.
—courtesy Ray Cabot

Sixth Street's finest

The last authentic crib left in Tombstone is located in the O.K. Corral.

Tombstone, 1879.
Fifth and Allen looking west

Grocery department of the Southwestern Commercial Company in Tombstone, Arizona.

The L.W. Blinn Lumber Company
—*The Tombstone prospector.*

California Variety Store in 1879.

Looking west on Allen Street in 1879.
Note crane at far right constructing the Cosmopolitan Hotel

Fremont Street.

Historical Photographs

The home of Jeff Milton still stands on the southeast corner of Third and Safford Streets in Tombstone. Milton was the last of the great lawmen in the area.

Tombstone Ore, 1881.
Wagons hauled Ore to the Stamp Mills on The San Pedro River.

The Tombstone stagecoach.

Historical Photographs

Quong Kee's famous Can-Can Restaurant.

Cummings & York Meat Market.

Historical Documents and Photographs of Tombstone

The old Tombstone Fire Station.
It still stands. A few feet to the right is the cave-in of the Million Dollar Stope.

Hose Team Number One, Tombstone, 1883.
Like other booming camps in the West, Tombstone was very proud of its Volunteer Fire Department.

Historical Photographs

The Final Resting Place of Ed Schieffelin

'NEATH this cairn of rocks, erected in the form of a giant prospector's discovery monument, rest the bones of Tombstone's founder, Ed Schieffelin. The monument, located about three miles west of the old mining camp, was erected by friends and associates of the great prospector.

Historical Documents and Photographs of Tombstone

THE OLD COURTHOUSE
If it could only talk!

TOMBSTONE'S COUNTY COURTHOUSE
before restoration witness to many famed trials and hangings! This Victorian was built in 1882 when the town was the County Seat, and many thought it soon would be the Territorial Capital. The carefully preserved exterior houses an extensive museum of area history, administered by the State Parks Board.

The Tombstone City Hall built in 1882.

Historical Photographs

The San Jose House located on the corner of Fremont and 5th Streets.

North side Allen Street between 4th & 5th Streets.

The first Post Office in Tombstone. on the corner of Fremont and Fourth Streets.

TOWN BAND lines up

apparently on some patriotic occasion in front of the Assay Office, Public Library and Epitaph Office, way back in the early days of the camp. This photo was taken on Fremont Street, just across from the City Hall.

Allen Street,
looking East from Fourth Street in 1902.
—Harper's Weekly, May 17, 1902

The Prospector and Tombstone Epitaph after they merged.

The Occidental Hotel
stood on Southeast corner of Allen and Fourth streets.

The "Can-Can" Restaurant owned by Kwong Kee and his partner, Ah Lum.

Nellie Cashman's Restaurant.

Historical Photographs

The Oriental Saloon.

The Oriental Saloon (on right), The Crystal Palace (center), looking East down Allen Street.

Moses and Wheeler Saloon, Tombstone, Arizona.

Historical Photographs

Gird Block
The front of Miner's Exchange on Fremont Street.

The Tombstone Epitaph Office, 1880.
At that time, the Epitaph Office had a balcony. Schieffelin Hall is seen on Fremont Street at the far right in this photo.

Historical Documents and Photographs of Tombstone

Virgil Earp's House
He lived at the corner of First and Fremont Streets, SW.

Pete Spencer's House
Located at the corner of First and Fremont Streets, SE.

The Alhambra Saloon

Depicted here are the elegant bar, sideboards, and fixtures of the Alhambra Saloon, reported in 1880 to have been the "boss" saloon establishment in Tombstone, Arizona. Thomas H. Corrigan, Owner of the Alhambra, constructed the elaborate bar of walnut, mahogany, and rosewoods, and furnished it with splendid sets of Bohemian, Italian, and French ware and the finest wines, liquors, and cigars. This illustration is a faithful engraving taken from a photograph by the well-known Tombstone photographer Camillus S. Fly.

Shaffer and Lord's General Mercantile

operated successfully in Tombstone and in the mining camps in neighboring Sonora.

Historical Documents and Photographs of Tombstone

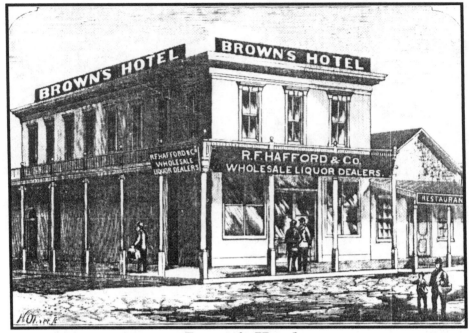

Brown's Hotel

The first hotel to be built in Tombstone. It was located at the corner of Fourth and Allen Streets. Adjoining the hotel, Owner Charles R. Brown leased business spaces to two storekeepers, and a number of one-story cottages to miners. This illustration was taken from an original photograph by C.S. Fly of Tombstone.

A city block of connecting store buildings, developed by Jim Vizina and Benjamin Cook.

Cornering at Fifth and Allen Streets in Tombstone, this modern structure housed the Safford, Hudson & Co. Bank; a first-class Saloon operated by M.E. Joyce; Charles Glover's Men's Clothing Store; and a dry goods store owned by L. Meyer.

Historical Photographs

Arcade Lodging House
(Now, the Rose Tree Inn).

El Papago Cash Store & City Hall, 1882.

Billy King's Saloon, 1895.

People's Store & Schieffelin Hall, 1885.

Historical Photographs

The first Wells Fargo Office in Tombstone.

Public School, Tombstone, Arizona.

Historical Documents and Photographs of Tombstone

City Marshal's Office, 1904

Pima County Bank & Smith's Mercantile, 1880.
(Now Visitor's Center)

Historical Photographs

Crystal Palace Saloon, 1882.

Campbell & Hatch Saloon
where Morgan Earp was killed, March 18, 1882.

View East on Allen Street; Tombstone, Arizona.

Tourist Hotel and Owl Cafe
Southeast corner, 5th & Allen.

View of the west side of 5th Street
between Allen & Fremont Streets.
The Epitaph Office now stands on this site.

The Gird Block.

Schieffelin Hall
as it appeared when Tombstone was at its lowest ebb. The building then, as now, houses the Masonic Lodge. Today it is beautifully restored.

Memorial Day Parade, Tombstone in 1882.
This photograph was taken by Cammilus S. Fly on Allen Street looking east from just below Third Street.

Historical Photographs

Doctor Goodfellow's home and office.

Cosmopolitan Hotel under construction 1879.

Bird Cage Theater as it stood abandoned.

Schieffelin Hall.

Sketch of the Bird Cage Theatre 1882.

The O.K. Corral
Shown as it appeared about the time the Railroad came to Tombstone.

Historical Photographs

The Disastrous Fire of 1881.

On June 22, 1881, C.S. Fly photographed the remains of the town. The sign of the O.K. Corral, amazingly was left standing!

Historical Documents and Photographs of Tombstone

SCHIEFFELIN HALL, May 25, 1882 at upper right, largest adobe building in the Southwest, still stands (and stands today) after Tombstone's second disastrous fire, May 25, 1882.

—Photo by C.S. Fly.

Building the railroad into Tombstone.

A miner and his family in Tombstone, 1880.

Building the railroad into Tombstone, 1902.

Gird Block, 1940.
Balcony at left was the Epitaph.

The Tombstone & Southern Railroad's first train.

Fire House for Engine Company No. 1.

Fire House corner Toughnut and Fifth Streets.

THE EPITAPH about 1915.

This photo was made during time the papers were owned by the Giragy family, when the office was still on Fremont Street across from the City Hall. Pictured, from left, are: George, Columbus, Mary and Carmel Giragi, Richard Dick, the "Brian Boy", and Orrin Preston.

The history of St. Paul's parallels Tombstone's.

THE O.K. CORRAL TODAY -

What tales these silent empty stalls could tell if they could talk ... but ... the battle site comes alive for visitors to Tombstone every first and third Sunday of every month when the town's famed Wild Bunch reenacts the shootout at the O.K. Corral - with such realism it's frightening to behold.

The losers in the Gunfight at O.K. Corral.

Historical Photographs

Buildings along Sixth Street in 1920 Tombstone

Historical Documents

Notice we the undersigned having discovered some mineral bearing quartz ledges which we are desirous under the provision of law to possess and work with a view to profit and ownership do in order to establish the locus of our claims and conform to the customs of the County hereby create a new mining district to be called the Tombstone Mining District, embracing within its boundaries all that portion of Pima County enclosed by the following lines, Commencing on the San Pedro River at a point opposite the old ruins and about eighteen miles above the upper crossing of the San Pedro River thence east to the western boundaries of the Dragoon Mountains, thence Southerly along the base of said mountains continuing the line to the Mule Mountains, Thence west to the San Pedro River. Thence Northerly down said river to the place of beginning, including all that range of Hills Known as the Tombstone Hills, together with their spurs. The Laws of Congress of the United States and of the Territory of Arizona, shall regulate the locating and holding of mining claims in this district with the exception that parties finding a mineral cropping shall be allowed thirty (30) days in which to establish and fix the boundaries of their claims. Dated April 5th 1878, in Tombstone District Pima County Arizona (Signed) A.E. Schieffelin, Richard Gird, E.L. Schieffelin, Oliver Boyer, Thos. E. Walker Filed and recorded at request of Richard Gird April 9th A.D. 1878 at 3 o'clock P.M.

S. W. Carpenter
County Recorder

Establishment of the Tombstone Mining District
April 5, 1878.

Richmond Town Site.

Notice is hereby given that on the 14th day of February A.D. 1879 we settled upon and improved as a Town Site and on the 20th day of March A.D. 1879 filed in the Land Office at Florence Arizona Declanitory Statement No 600 for the following described as follows situated in Tombstone Mining District County of Pima Territory of Arizona. Commencing at the North West corner of the Lucky Cuss Mining Claim and running Northerly 880 yards along the West boundary line of the Old Guard Mining Claim to a stake, thence Westerly 880 yards to a stake, thence Southerly 880 yards to a stake, thence Easterly 880 yards to the place of beginning in the district of lands subject to sale at the Land Office at Florence Arizona, and containing 160 acres And we do hereby claim said land as a Town Site for the Town of Richmond and under Section 2388 of the Revised Statutes of the United States.

Alphens Lewis
John B. Kern
Robert A. Lewis

Comprising Richmond Town Company

Filed and Recorded at request of A Lewis March 21st 1879 at 1:35 P.M.

S. W. Carpenter County Recorder
By W. A. McDermott Deputy

Richmond Town site established February 14, 1879.

Historical Documents and Photographs of Tombstone

Territory of Arizona,
County of ~~Yavapai~~ Pima } ss.

I, V. W. Earp, do solemnly swear that I will support the Constitution of the United States and the laws of this Territory; that I will true faith and allegiance bear to the same, and defend them against all enemies whatsoever, and that I will faithfully and impartially discharge the duties of the office of Deputy United States Marshal according to the best of my abilities, so help God.

V W Earp

Sworn and subscribed to before me this 27th day of November A. D. 1879

U.S. Dist Clerk

Sworn statement of Virgil Earp.

Sign in front of the Crystal Palace Saloon.

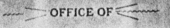

Parsons & Redfern business announcement.

In the Justice's Court of _____ **Township,**
No. 159

of the _____ of _____ County of _____

	Action	
vs. Plaintiff	Demand $	
		Attorney for Plaintiff
Defendant		Attorney for Defendant

DATE	PROCEEDINGS

Record of Marriages

I certify that on the 6th day of July 1880 at Tombstone, the County of Pima, Territory of Arizona, N. F. Leslie and May Killeen both of Tombstone, said county, were by me joined in marriage.

James Reilly J.P.

Witnesses
C. F. Hine
Louisa Bilicke

I certify that on this 19th day of September 1880 at Tombstone in the County of Pima, Arizona Territory, Jacob Endlich and Anne H. Finnerey both of Tombstone A.T. were by me joined in the holy bonds of matrimony.

James Reilly J.P.

Witness
John J. Deenee

I certify that on this 25th day of September 1880, August Barone and Christine Schaeffer both of Tombstone A.T. were by me joined in the holy bonds of matrimony.

James Reilly J.P. of Precinct #17 Pima County A.T.

Witness John Buettner
H. Al. Sheifflin

Record of Marriages.
Entries include N. F. Leslie and May Killeen.

LOT NO. 62

Field Notes

of the survey of the

1st North Extension of the Mountain Maid Mining Claim

Situate in _____ Tombstone _____ mining district,

County of _____ Pima _____ and in Sec. 2-11, Tp. 20S.,

Range 22E, of the Gila and Salt River Meridian,

ARIZONA.

Claimed by _____ N.W. Earp, W.S. Earp, J.C. Earp and R.J. Winders _____

Survey executed by _____ H.G. Howe _____ D. S.,

Under instructions dated _____ November 10th _____ 1880

Survey commenced _____ November 13th _____ 1880
Survey completed _____ November 15th _____ 1880

Mine Property Survey.

Historical Documents and Photographs of Tombstone

FINAL OATHS FOR SURVEYS OF MINING CLAIMS & MILL SITES.

A LIST of the names of individuals employed to assist in running, measuring, or working the lines and corners described in the foregoing field-notes of the survey of the 1st North Extension of the Mountain Maid, Mining Claim, is in Tombstone. _____ Mining District, Pima _____ County, Arizona, showing the respective capacities in which they acted.

R. J. Winders. Chainman.
Thomas Kelley, Chainman.
Wyatt Earp. Flagman.

WE hereby certify that we assisted Henry G. Howe, U. S. Deputy Surveyor, in surveying the 1st North Extension of the Mountain Maid Mining Claim, claimed by V.W. Earp, W.S. Earp, J.C. Earp and R.J. Winders, located in Tombstone _____ Mining District, Pima _____ County, and in Township No. _____ Range No. _____ of the Gila and Salt River base and meridian, Arizona, and that said Survey has been in all respects, to the best of our knowledge and belief, well and faithfully executed, and the boundary monuments planted according to the instructions furnished by the Surveyor General.

R. J. Winders, Chainman.
Thomas Kelley, Chainman.
_____ Axeman.
Wyatt Earp Flagman.

SWORN TO AND SUBSCRIBED before me this 16th day of November, 1880.

Henry G. Howe,
Notary Public, Pima County A. T.

I, Henry G. Howe, U. S. Deputy Surveyor, do solemnly swear that, in pursuance of instructions from John Wasson, U. S. Surveyor-General for Arizona, bearing date the 10th day of November, 1880, I have well, faithfully and truly, in my own proper person, and in strict conformity with the instructions furnished by the Surveyor-General and the laws of the United States, surveyed all those portions of the 1st North Extension of the Mountain Maid Mining Claim, claimed by V.W. Earp, W.S. Earp, J.C. Earp and R.J. Winders _____ Tombstone _____ Mining District, Pima _____ County, _____ as are represented in the foregoing field-notes of the said survey, all under my directions, I do further solemnly swear that all the corners of said survey have been established and perpetuated in strict accordance with the instructions furnished me, and that the foregoing are the true and original field notes of said survey.

Henry G. Howe, Deputy Surveyor.

SWORN TO AND SUBSCRIBED before me this 16th day of November 1880.

W. H. Harwood
Notary Public

Final Oaths for Surveys of Mining Claims and Millsites regarding the Mountain Maid Mining Claim.

AFFIDAVIT OF FIVE HUNDRED DOLLARS IMPROVEMENTS.

We, George Mely and J. H. Holliday of lawful age, being first duly sworn according to law, depose and say that we are acquainted with the Work done upon and improvements made upon the 1st N Ext. of the Mountain Maid, mining claim, situate in Tombstone _____ Mining District, Pima County, Arizona Territory, for which V. W. Earp, W. S. Earp and J. Earp, and R. J. Winders has made application for survey prior to application for patent under the provisions of the Act of Congress approved May 10, 1872, and that the labor done and improvements made thereon by the applicant and grantor exceed Five Hundred Dollars in value, and further that we are not personally interested in said mine.

George Mely
J. H. Holliday

TERRITORY OF ARIZONA, } SS.
County of Pima.

SWORN AND SUBSCRIBED before me this 16th day of November, 1880.

James Reilly
Notary Public

Doc Holliday witnessed the $500 improvements on The Mountain Maid Mine.

Certification of post mortem
conducted on the body of Chas Storms.

Tombstone, A.T. Sept 4th 1880.

The County of Pima, Territory of Arizona

Dr. To James Anderson.

For services as guard for fourteen nights @ $5.00 per night, amounting to Seventy Dollars. Co $70.00

J. W. Anderson

Charles A. Shibell Sheriff
by Wyatt Earp
Deputy Sheriff

I hereby certify that the above bill is correct and was rendered by above claimant in the case of Territory of Arizona, County of Pima vs. Geo. Perine.

Wyatt Earp

A bill for Guard Services.

Historical Documents and Photographs of Tombstone

Know all men by these presents that I Charles A. Shibell Sheriff of the County of Pima Territory of Arizona do hereby appoint Wyatt S. Earp of the town of Tombstone in said County a Deputy Sheriff in and for said Pima County.

In witness whereof I have hereunto set my hand this 27th day of July 1880.

                                Charles A. Shibell
                                Sheriff Pima Co. A.T.

Territory of Arizona } ss
County of Pima }

I, Wyatt S. Earp do solemnly swear that I will support the Constitution of the United States and the laws of this Territory; that I will true faith and allegiance bear to the same, and defend them against all Enemies whatsoever, and that I will faithfully and impartially discharge the duties of the Office of Deputy Sheriff of Pima County according to the best of my abilities. So help me God.

Sworn and subscribed to before me this 27th July 1880

   M. Gray   W. S. Earp

Justice No. 17
Pima County
Arizona

Wyatt Earp's oath of office as Pima County Deputy Sheriff.

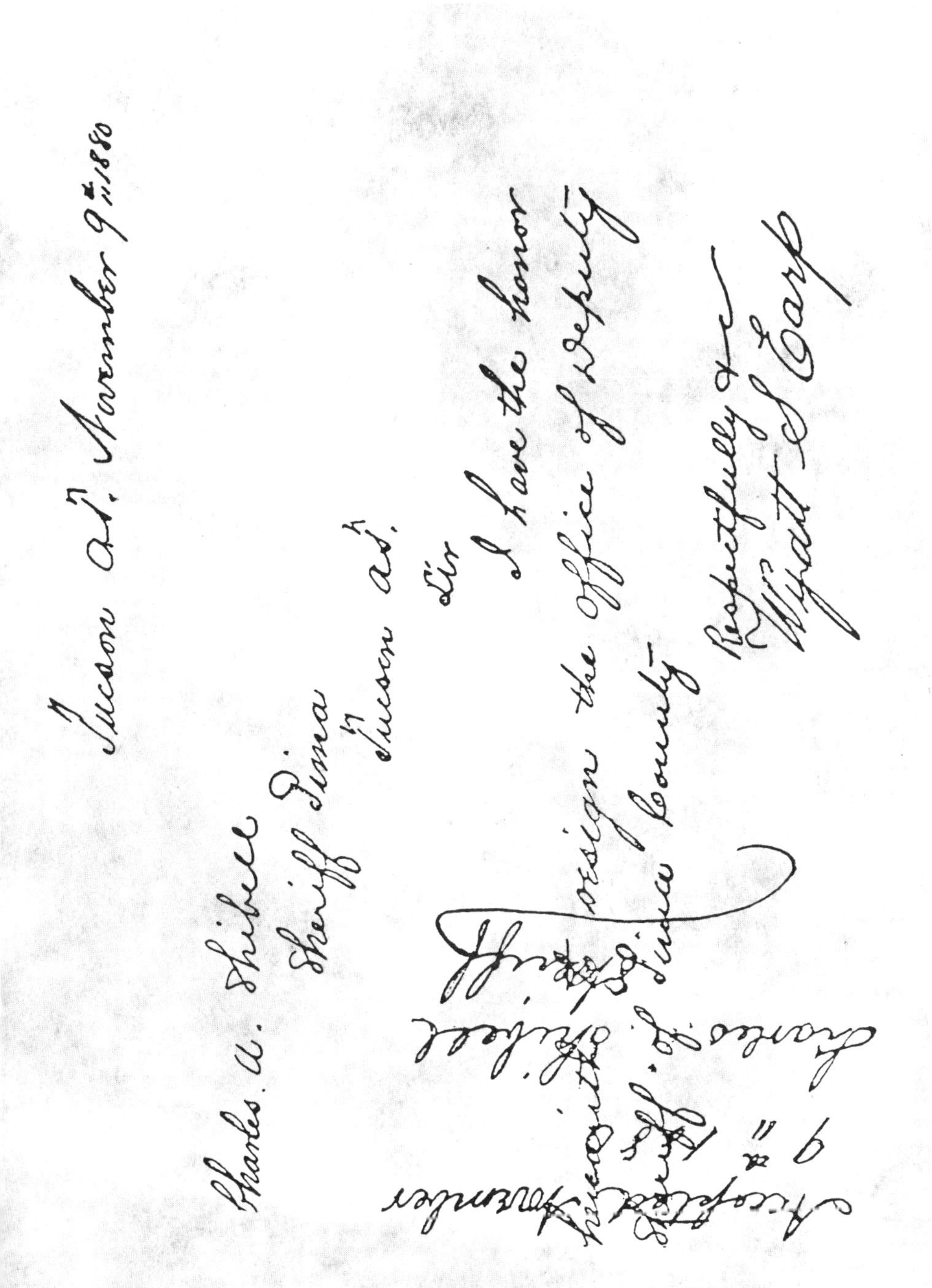

Historical Documents

Tucson A.T. November 9th 1880

Charles A. Shibell
Sheriff Pima
Tucson A.T.

Sir

I have the honor to resign the office of deputy sheriff Pima County—

Respectfully yours
Wyatt S. Earp

Accepted November 9" th
Charles A. Shibell
Sheriff

The resignation of Wyatt S. Earp as Deputy Sheriff.

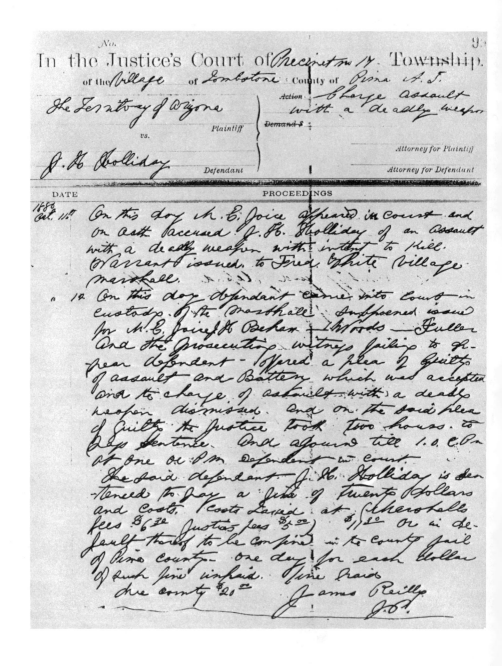

Joyce accuses J. H. Holliday.

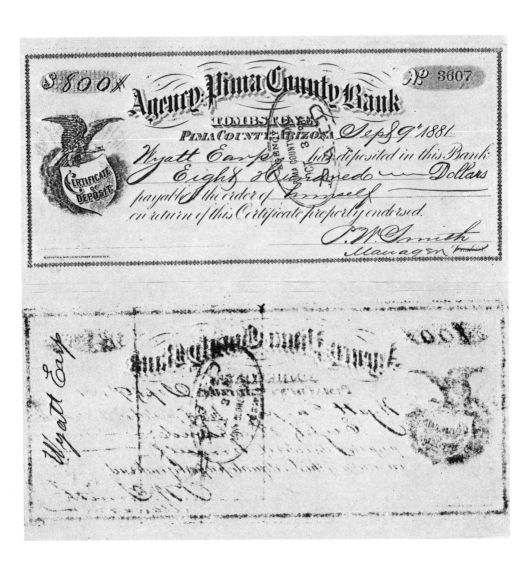

Deposit Receipt for $800.

NO. _____

IN THE RECORDER'S COURT, CITY OF TOMBSTONE,
CACHISE COUNTY, TERRITORY OF ARIZONA.

Before A. O. Wallace, Recorder

The Mayor and Common Council of the City of Tombstone, Plaintiffs.

v.

Wyatt Earp

Defendant

188_

DATE	PROCEEDINGS
June 19"	The Mayor and Common Council of the City of Tombstone v. Wyatt Earp. Complaint laid before me by Chief of Police V. W. Earp charging defendant with disturbing the peace and fighting in violation of an ordinance. Defendant arrested and brought in Court by said officer and plead guilty and after due deliberation had thereon it is ordered and adjudged by the Court, now here, that the defendant be fined in the sum of Twenty dollars. Fine paid and defendant discharged. Recorders fees $5.00

A. O. Wallace
Recorder.

Complaint against Wyatt Earp.

Historical Documents

CRIMINAL REGISTER OF ACTIONS.

THE TERRITORY OF ARIZONA,
vs.

J. H. Holliday
Defendant

Felony
Indictment found
May 27th 1881

Lyttleton Price
For the Terr.

A. G. P. George
Defendant's Attorney

PROCEEDINGS HAD.	Dr.	Cr.	DISPOSITION OF CAUSE.
May 27 Indictment for Felony filed	25		Continued for term.
" Entering Cause	1 00		May 8th —
" Certified Copy of indictment	1 50		Bond forfeited.
" Entering Cause on Calendar	1 00		
" Order of Continuance for term	1 00		
R. R. to C —	4 75		
July 7 Cr By County Warrant		4 75	
	$4 75	$4 75	
Nov 18 To Entering cause on Calendar	2 00		B.R.
" " Iss. 3 Subpoenas	3 00 √		
6 " 3 "	3 00 √		
1882			
" 21 Filing "	2 00 B.R.		
By Settlement		6 00 √	On motion of Dist
May 6 To Ent. Cause on Calendar	2 00		Atty ordered stricken
			Calendar. Nov 13. '82
	$12 00		
Nov 1 Ent on Calendar	2 00 √		
13 Motion and Order	2 00		

Fees Settled

Criminal Register of Actions in an indictment of J. H. "Doc" Holliday.

"In accordance with the Ordinances of the Christian Church and the laws of Arizona Mr. Spencer Clawson and Miss Lois I. Brown both of Tombstone were by me United in the bonds of Matrimony in Tombstone Arizona on the 14th of August 1881.

Witness } I.H. Puttle Elder of M.E.C.
H.M. Mathews }

Filed and recorded at request of I.H. Puttle. aug 16, 1881. at 11.15 am

A.I. Jones
County Recorder

Territory of Arizona } ss. This is to certify that the
County of Cochise } undersigned a Justice of the Peace of said County did on the 12th day of August A.D. 1881. at the City of Tombstone join in lawful wedlock Peter Spencer and Maria Duarte with their mutual consent in presence of.

Witnesses } A.O. Wallace
Alejandro Olguin } Justice of the Peace
George Moore

Filed and recorded at request of A.O. Wallace aug.13, 1881, at. 3 P.M.

A.I. Jones
County Recorder.

Territory of Arizona } ss
" County of Cochise } This is to certify that on this 23d day of August before me. Wells Spicer. a Justice of the Peace in and for said County personally came Mr. A Yak & Miss Ty By who being of suitable age and condition for matrimony and there being no objection thereto they were by me Joined and united in the bonds of marriage

Marriages Book, Peter Spencer to Maria Duarte. etc.

Territory of Arizona
County of Cochise } ss

I John P. Clum do solemnly swear that I will support the Constitution of the United States, the laws of this Territory, and the laws and ordinances governing the city of Tombstone, that I will true faith and allegiance bear to the same, and defend them against all enemies whatsoever, and that I will faithfully and impartially discharge the duties of the office of Mayor of the city of Tombstone and Territory of Arizona, according to the the best of my abilities so help me God.

Sworn and subscribed to before me this   day of January AD 1881

John P. Clum

A. O. Wallace
Justice of the Peace

John P. Clum's oath of office
as Mayor of Tombstone.

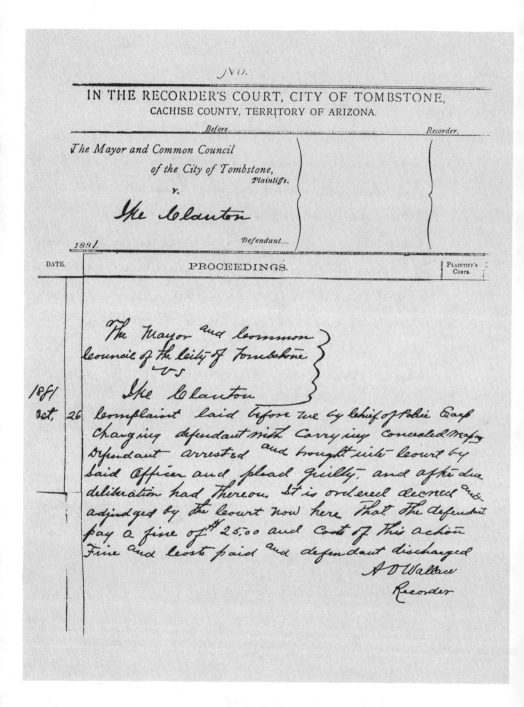

Recording of the complaint against Ike Clanton.

Historical Documents

Territory of Arizona }
County of Cochise }

I hereby certify that since the within return was made on the accompanying writ of Habeas Corpus I have received a writ of commitment and now hold the said J H Holliday, Wyatt Earp and Morgan Earp under and by virtue of said writ of commitment, a copy of which is hereunto annexed.

J H Behan, Sheriff
By H M Woods
Under Sheriff

Tombstone, Feb 15, 1882

(Copy of Warrant of Commitment

Territory of Arizona }
County of Cochise }

The within named J. H. Holliday, Wyatt Earp and Morgan Earp having been brought before me under this warrant, are committed for examination to the Sheriff of Cochise County, Arizona Territory — this February 15th, 1882

J B Smith
Justice of the Peace in and for Cochise County

Behan rearrested Wyatt Earp, Doc Holliday and Morgan Earp.

Historical Documents and Photographs of Tombstone

Among others, is a Check made to John Slaughter for $1,000.

Historical Documents

Certificate from O.K. Corral
owners "Honest" John Montgomery and Mr. Benson. The stable owned by these men was the sight of the famous gunfight.

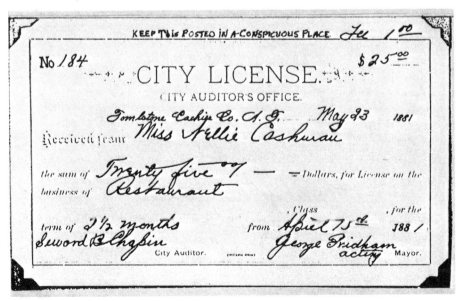

City License issued to Miss Nellie Cashman.

Historical Documents and Photographs of Tombstone

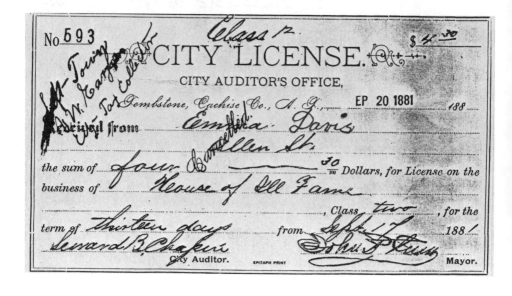

Note that the above left town and the below refused payment and that both notations are signed by V. W. Earp, City tax collector.

Licenses for Houses of Ill Fame.

Historical Documents

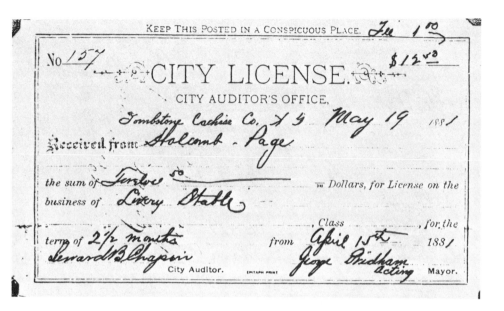

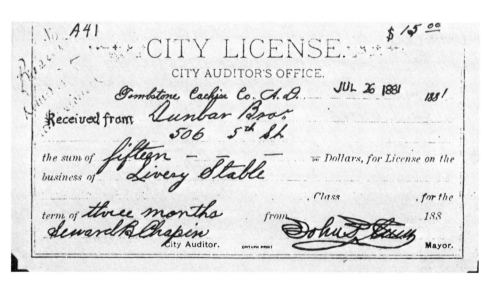

*These City Licenses were issued for Livery Stables,
(top) to Holcomb; (bottom) to Dunbar Bros.*

Tombstone A.T.
Jan 14th 1881

Colts Patent F. A. Com

Gentlemen
    I want a pistol made as follows,
  Colts Frontier Model to take Winchester Cartridges 44 Cal, the revolver to have a twelve (12) inch barrel, browned, superior finished throughout with carved Ivory handle, also send Scabberd or belt with every thing Complete for Carrying & Cleaning. the Pistol answer soon as Convenient, stating price and when I can have Pistol by Wells Fargo & Cos, and oblige
    Yours Respt
    Capt N.H. Leslie
    Box 28.
    Tombstone
    Arizona, Territory

P.S. I want this Pistol to be first class in every respect.
N.H. Leslie

Request to Colts for a pistol.

Historical Documents

IN THE RECORDER'S COURT, CITY OF TOMBSTONE
CACHISE COUNTY, TERRITORY OF ARIZONA.

Before A. O. Wallace, Rec...

Mayor and Common Council
of the City of Tombstone,
  Plaintiffs.
  v.
W. Claybourne
  Defendant

1881

DATE	PROCEEDINGS
June 7	Complaint laid before me June 7/81 by Officer Cornelison charging defendant with being drunk and disorderly in violation of our City ordinance. Defendant arrested and brought in Court by said officer, plead guilty, and after due consideration had thereon it is ordered and adjudged by the Court now here that defendant be fined in the sum seven and 50/100 dollars including the costs of this action taxed & in default of the payment of such fine he be confined & imprisoned in the City jail for the period of four days. Fine paid and defendant discharged. Recorders fee $5.00 under fine 2.50 A. O. Wallace Recorder

Complaint brought against W. Claybourne.

Historical Documents and Photographs of Tombstone

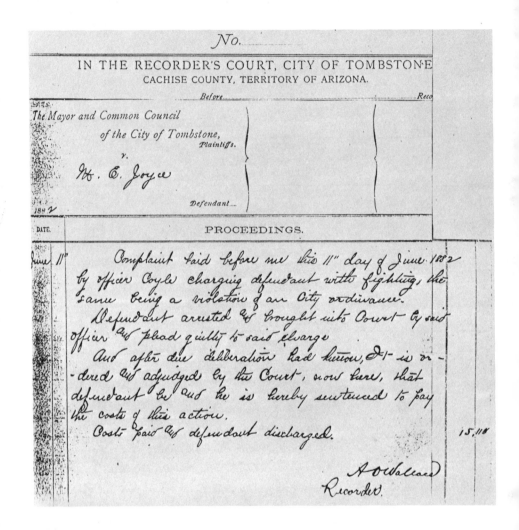

Claim brought against Mr. E. Joyce by Officer Coyle.

Historical Documents

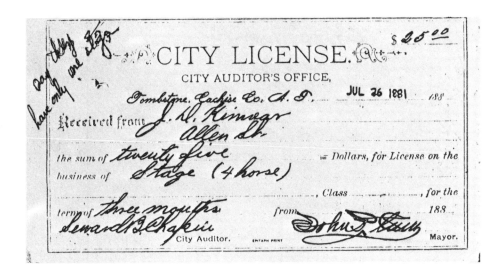

J. D. Kinnear stage License.

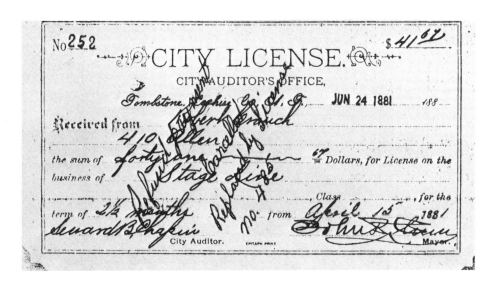

Robert Crouch was called Sandy Bob.

> City of Tombstone
> To Morgan Earp   Dr
> to five days Work as Special
> Policeman in the month of
> Sept 1881 — — $20.00
>
>   V. W. Earp
>   Chief of Police
>
> Bill of
> Morgan Earp   Morgan Earp
> $20.00
>
>   Filed.   OCT 3 1881
>   Read.   OCT. 17 1881
>   Approved OCT 17
>   Paid   OCT. 18 1881
>   Warrant, No. 26

An Authorization to pay Morgan Earp.

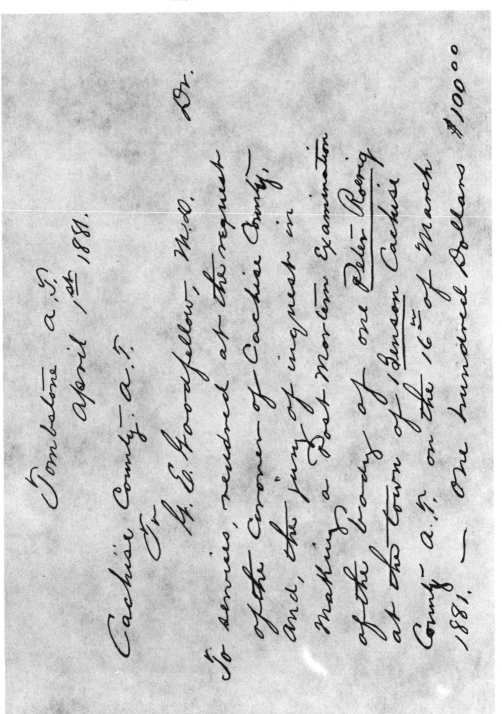

Bill from Dr. George E. Goodfellow.

No.

IN THE RECORDER'S COURT, CITY OF TOMBSTONE,
CACHISE COUNTY, TERRITORY OF ARIZONA.

Before _____ Recorder _____

The Mayor and Common Council
of the City of Tombstone,
         Plaintiffs.
    v.
Charles Fay
         Defendant.

PROCEEDINGS.

Complaint laid before me this 19th day of September 1882, by Officer Coyle charging the defendant with fighting, the same being a violation of an City Ordinance. Defendant arrested and brought into Court by said officer and plead guilty to said charge and after due deliberation had thereon It is ordered and adjudged by the Court now here that defendant leave the City, that if he be found within the City by 5 P.M. that he be then brought in and committed to jail for 5 days

         A O Wallace
         Recorder

The Mayor and Common Council
of the City of Tombstone
    v.
Frank Leslie

Complaint laid before me this 28th of Sept 1882 by Officer Poynton, charging deft with carrying and brandishing a deadly weapon the same being, then and there, a violation of an City ordinance. Defendant arrested and brought into Court by said officer and pleads guilty to said charge and after due deliberation had thereon, It is Ordered and adjudged by the Court now here, that deft be and he is hereby sentenced to pay the costs of this action amounting to sixteen dollars. Costs paid and defendant discharged.

         A O Wallace
         Recorder

Complaint against Charles Fay and Frank Leslie.

City of Tombstone

Virgil W. Earp
To
The Mayor and Common Council of the City of Tombstone

Bond

Upon examination of the within I find the same correct I therefore approve the same

Marcus R. Ryan
City attorney

Territory of Arizona } ss
County of Cochise } I Virgil W Earp do solemnly swear that I will support the constitution of the U.S. and the Laws of this Territory, the Charter and Ordinances Rules, and By Laws governing the City of Tombstone, and that I will true faith and allegiance bear to the same and defend them from all enemies whatsoever and that I will faithfully and impartially discharge the duties of the office of Chief of Police of the City of Tombstone according to the best of my abilities so help me God

Sworn and subscribed to before me this 24th day of June A.D. 1881.

Leonard B. Chapin
Clerk of Council

V. W. Earp.

The Sworn Statement of Virgil W. Earp.

Regular November Term AD 1881

Territory of Arizona
 Plaintiff
vs
John Ringgold
 Defendant

Indictment for Felony.

The defendant was brought into Court. and the District Attorney being present and Robinson and Goodrich appearing as Counsel for the defendant — the defendant was asked if John Ringgold was his true name to which he replied that it was not. and that his true name was John Ringo. whereupon the Court ordered the indictment corrected. The indictment charging the defendant with the crime of Robbery was then read to him by the Clerk. and a plea of Not Guilty was entered by the defendant and a true Copy of the indictment was handed to him.
The defendant was then given one day to prepare for trial.

An Indictment for Felony.

Territory of Arizona
    Plaintiff
       vs
John Ringo
    Defendant

Indictment for Robbery

This being the day set for the arraignment of the defendant. The defendant was brought into Court — and the District Attorney and Ben Goodrich Esq. of Counsel for defendant — being in Court — the defendant was asked if John Ringo was his true name — to which he replied that it was. The indictment charging him with the crime of Robbery was then read to him and a true copy thereof was given to him ———

Court Record, indictment of John Ringo.

CRIMINAL REGISTER OF ACTIONS.

THE TERRITORY OF ARIZONA, vs.

Defendant: John Ringgold

Robbery
Indictment found Nov 26th 1881

Lyttleton Price, For the Territory
Goodrich & Goodrich, Defendant's Attorney

Date	PROCEEDINGS HAD.	Dr.	Cr.	DISPOSITION OF CAUSE.
Nov 29	Entering Cause	1 00		Admitted to Bail
"	Filing Indictment	25		Dec 1st 1881 under
"	Cert Copy "	1 00		Indictment of Nov 29-81
"	Issuing Bench Warrant	1 00		
30	Filing	1 05		
Dec ~~4~~	~~To trial of Cause~~	~~5 00~~		
" 2	Copy Indictment	~~1 00~~		Transferred to Page 81
" "	~~Filing~~	~~25~~		
"	Issuing 6 Subpoenas	6 00		
17	Filing	1 00		B.R.
24	Iss. order for rearrest	1 00 BR.		Jany 24th 1882
Jany 5	By County Warrant		1.00	Bond declared by Court
11	To Ent caus on Calendar	2 00		insufficient & Sheriff
"	Trial of Cause Dismissal	5 00		directed to rearrest
"	Ent Judgt.	1 00		defendant
		$20 25		May 8th Set for
				Trial May 12th
				May 18th Cause
				dismissed Defendant
				Bail exonerated

Fur Settled

Territory of Arizona Plaintiff
vs
John Ringo Defendant

Indictment for Robbery

This being the day set for the arraignment of the defendant. The defendant was brought into Court – and the District Attorney and Ben Goodrich Esq. of Counsel for defendant – being in Court – the defendant was asked if John Ringo was his true name – to which he replied that it was. The indictment charging him with the crime of Robbery was then read to him and a true copy thereof was given to him – –

Arraignment of John Ringo.

Historical Documents and Photographs of Tombstone

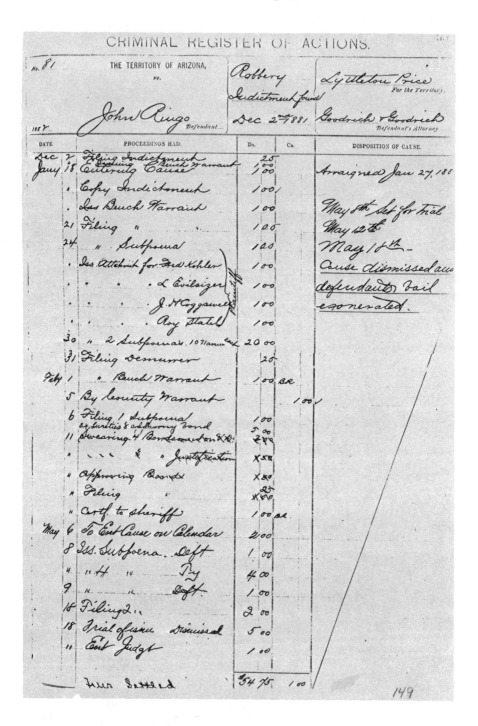

Criminal Register of Actions.

Ordinance No 31

The <u>Mayor</u> and <u>Common Council</u> of the City of Tombstone, Territory of Arizona, do <u>ordain</u> as follows.

That <u>section 64</u> of <u>Chapter 17</u> of the <u>Code of Ordinances</u> of the City of Tombstone, approved August 30th 1881 <u>be amended</u> to read as follows

Sec. 64 - Every person keeping a house or room of Ill Fame, in which one or more persons are inmates, shall pay a monthly license of ten dollars and every person keeping such house where wine, malt or spirituous liquors are sold, shall pay a monthly license of twenty dollars.

S. B. Chapin
Clerk

V. A. Gregg
City Attorney

Approved December 8th 1881

John P. Clum
Mayor

John P. Clum
Mayor

Attest
S. B. Chapin
Clerk

City Ordinance of Tombstone.

Grand Ball Program.

Historical Documents

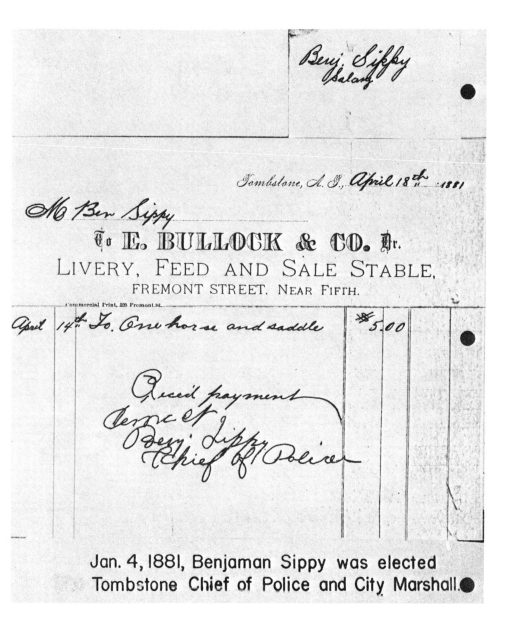

Jan. 4, 1881, Benjaman Sippy was elected Tombstone Chief of Police and City Marshall.

Receipt for Payment.

Charleston, Arizona
Feb. 14th 1882

Billy Byers
Leavenworth
    Dear Billy
Your letter of the 8th was duly
Received — was truly pleased to hear
hear from you Every thing is
Runing Satisfactory this way
I have got the Earps all in Jail
and am not going to unhitch
I have got them on the
hip and am going to throw
them good — Tim sends his
kind Regards — Frank has
finally gone to Gorgia Jeff
Lewis address Colorado City Tex
Excuse this short note I will
try to pitty Sowes Com plour
and all these kind of things.
            Ike Clanton

*Letter from Ike Clanton
to Billy Byers in Leavenworth.*

> Territory of Arizona } ss.
> County of Cochise }
>
> Nellie Cashman being duly sworn says on oath that the receipts taken by her monthly in Conducting the American Hotel on Fremont St in Tombstone are less than one thousand dollars per month.
>
> Subscribed and sworn to
>
> Nellie Cashman
>
> before me this 12th day of June 1882
>
> B O'Quigley
> Notary Public

The sworn statement of Nellie Cashman.

Know all men by these presents
That we Virgil W. Earp as prin
-cipal and J. M. Vizina
and C. R. Brown as
sureties are held and firmly bound
unto the Mayor and Common
Council of the City of Tombstone,
Cochise County, Territory of Arizo-
-na in the full sum of Five
thousand Dollars, for the payment of which said sum well
and truly to be made we bind
ourselves our heirs our executors
and administrators jointly and
severally, firmly by these presents.
Sealed with our seals and
dated this 29th day of June
A.D. 1881.
The condition of the above
obligation is such that whereas
the above named principal
Virgil W. Earp has been appoint
-ed by the Mayor and Common
Council of the City of Tombstone
of the Territory of Arizona to the
Office of Chief of Police in and
for said City of Tombstone Terri
-tory aforesaid for the term specified in
the Charter. Now Therefore the condition

Virgil Earps' bond as Chief of Police.

of this obligation is such that if the said Virgil W. Earp shall well and truly and faithfully perform all official duties now required of him by law, ordi=nance, rule resolution or regu=lation, and shall promptly true and faithfully pay to said City all moneys that may come into his hands belonging to said City, and shall well, truly and faithfully execute and perform all the duties of said Office of Chief of Police or any other position to which he may be appointed by said Mayor and Common Council of said City to be required of him by any law, ordinance, resolution, rule or regulation to be enacted or passed subsequently to the exe=cution of this bond, then this obligation to be void and of no effect otherwise to remain in full force and virtue

Signed sealed and V. W. Earp
delivered in the presence of J. M. Vizina
Marcus R. Hayne C. R. Brown

Earp-Clanton Murder Case. Document No. 94.

In Justice Court, Tombstone No. 1, Cochise County, Arizona Territory.

Territory of Arizona)
)
       vs   ) Deposition
)
Morgan Earp, et al)

On this 11th day of November, 1881, on the hearing of the above entitled cause, on the examination of Wyatt Earp and J. H. Holliday, Dr. H. M. Matthews, a witness of lawful age, being produced and sworn, deposes and says the following:

Territory of Arizona)
) ss
County of Cochise   )

Dr. H. M. Matthews. Nov. 11. Questioned about the pistols "now before the court." A. Says he picked one up from beside the -- lying close by--the body of Frank McLoury. The other was given to him (the) next day by Mr. Fly, as property of Wm. Clanton. Points to one with two loads in it as that of Frank McLoury. Is questioned about testimony of Thos. Keefe, regarding pistol on floor, and says he laid it there while he examined the body of Tom (McLoury) and that it was the same pistol he had picked up from beside Frank McLoury. Says he received no other arms.

                     Cross Ex.

It is brought out that the only information the doctor had about "Wm. Clanton's pistol" was that it was so designated by Mr. Fly. Other involved questions are ask and overruled. Defense moves to strike out "property of Wm. Clanton." Overruled. Here the pistols are examined as to numbers on them, "and the one with four empty chambers indentified by witness Keofe as being found by him on the floor in the house . . . . is numbered 46338 and the cylinder is numbered 6338 and is the same pistol identified by Dr. Matthews as found by him near the body of Frank McLoury, and the other pistol identified by Dr. Matthew as given him by Mr. Fly is numbered 52196 and the cylinder is 2196.

                (Sig.) H. M. Matthews

                H M Matthews
             Coroner Cochise Co. a.t.

Deposition relating to the Earp-Clanton Murder Case.

Historical Documents

Register of Actions and Fee Book, District Court

No. 154

In the matter of the inquest held on the body of

Year 1881

Frank McLowery, Deceased.

Inquest held by

H. M. Matthews, Coroner.

PROCEEDINGS. | DR. | CR.

Oct 26 — Inquest held
Dec 1 — Filed.
Cause of death, "gun shot wounds"
(See inquest papers of Wm. Clanton.)

No. 155

In the matter of the inquest held on the body of

1881

Thomas McLowery, Deceased.

Inquest held by

H. M. Matthews, Coroner.

PROCEEDINGS. | DR. | CR.

Oct 26 — Inquest held
Dec 1 — Filed.
Cause of death, "gun shot wounds"
(See inquest papers in Clanton case.)

Register of Actions and Fee Book
District Court showing causes of death of Frank and Thomas McLaury (shown here as McLowery).

Inquest Report
concerning the body of Wm (Billy) Clanton

Inquest Report
concerning the body of William Claibourne.

Historical Documents

1st Judicial District, Cochise County, Arizona

No. 170

In the matter of the Inquest held on the body of

Jul 1882 — John Ringo, Deceased

Inquest held by Citizens, Coroner

PROCEEDINGS

June 14 — Inquest held.
Nov 3 — Filed.
Cause of death, "unknown" But supposed gunshot wounds.

Inquest Report
concerning the body of John Ringo.

No. 70

In the matter of the Inquest held on the body of

Mar 1889 — Mollie Edwards alias Leslie, Deceased

Inquest held by J. C. Easton, Coroner

PROCEEDINGS

July 12 — Inquest held.
31 — Filed.
Cause of death, "pistol shot wounds."

Inquest Report
concerning Mollie Edwards

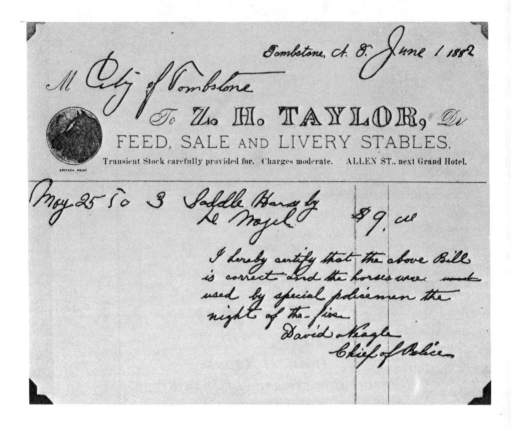

Certification of Bill.

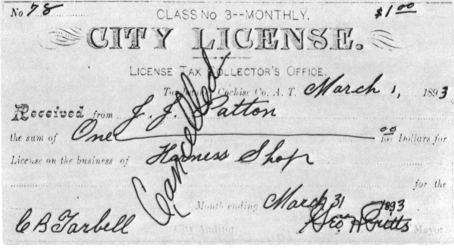

Monthly City License cancelled.

Historical Documents

Mr. G. H. Swain
And Ladies are Cordially invited to Attend a Social Dance to be Given by
THE TOMBSTONE STAGS
At Mining Exchange Hall on the Evening of February 21st, 1896.
COMMITTEE

Social Dance Invitation.

EXECUTION OF
DANIEL KELLY, OMER W. SAMPLE, JAS. HOWARD, DANIEL DOWD and WILLIAM DELANEY,
AT THE COURT HOUSE, TOMBSTONE, ARIZONA,
March 28, 1884, at 1 O'clock p. m.
Admit Mr. G. H. Swain
NOT TRANSFERABLE. J. L. Ward, SHERIFF.

Ticket
to the execution of
Bisbee Massacre killers.

Tombstone, Ariz. July 28, 1900.
Mr. Geo. W. Swain
The Sheriff of Cochise County, Arizona, announces that on Friday, August 10, 1900, at the hour of 12 o'clock, Noon.
WILLIAM HALDERMAN.
AND
THOMAS HALDERMAN.
Will be Executed at the Jail Yard in this City, for the Murder of Teddy Moore. You are Respectfully Invited to Witness the Execution.
Scott White
SHERIFF.

Announcement
for the execution of the
Haldermans.

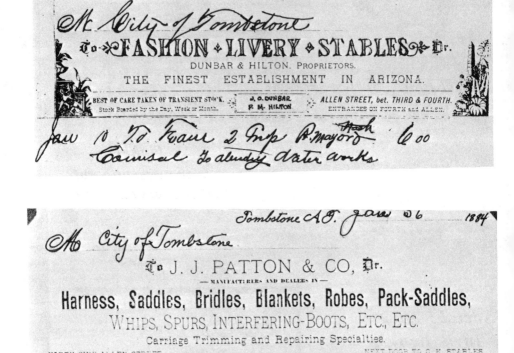

Livery receipts.

In the District Court Cochise Co. Ary.

City of Tombstone
vs.
D. H. McNeil
deft.
} Involving question
of title to city
water works

For the fee of $250.00 net. I agree to assist the City Attorney in the trial of above case in said District Court & in the preparation of the Brief & papers on appeal in the Supreme Court of said Territory, Said City to pay all expenses of both trial & appeal - printing briefs & costs of court & clerk - and should the City desire my personal presence at the hearing in said Supreme Court there said City to pay my actual expenses of such trip.

August 3d 1889.

Allen R. English

Allen R. English
defends title of city.

Epitaph printer's bill.

Historical Documents

IN THE RECORDER'S COURT, CITY OF TOMBSTONE
CACHISE COUNTY, TERRITORY OF ARIZONA.

Before _____

The Mayor and Common Council of the City of Tombstone, Plaintiffs.

v.

Eugene _____ Defendant

} Failing to procure a license.

1885

DATE.	PROCEEDINGS.
Nov 19	Defendant was charged upon the sworn complaint of Daniel O'Connor with conducting a house of ill fame without procuring a license. Defendant was brought into court upon a warrant and plead guilty. Fined ten dollars and costs amounting to twenty-four dollars. Defendant paid ten dollars and was committed for the balance. _John _____ Recorder_
	Mayor and Common Council vs. Dr. G. E. Goodfellow } Failure to procure license.
Nov 23	Defendant was charged upon the sworn complaint of Daniel O'Connor with conducting the profession of a physician and surgeon without procuring a license. Defendant came into court and plead not guilty and upon examination was discharged. _John _____ Recorder_

Failing to procure a license

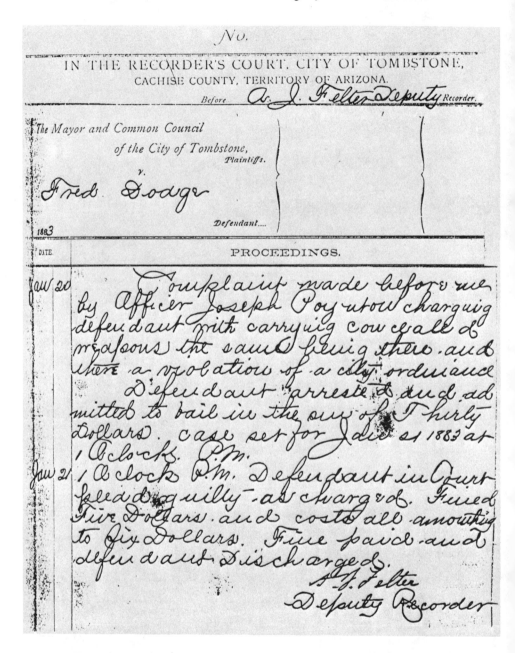

Fred Dodge, violation of a City Ordinance.

IN THE RECORDER'S COURT, CITY OF TOMBSTONE
COCHISE COUNTY, TERRITORY OF ARIZONA

The Territory of Arizona,
Plaintiff,
vs.
West Fuller,
Defendant.

Charge: Felonious Assault. Committed in Tombstone.

PROCEEDINGS.

2nd. On this day Rosario Gonzales made complaint on oath and in writing accusing the above named West Fuller of assault with a deadly weapon to wit Brass Knuckles one Juan Alverez with intent to commit a bodily injury on the person of said Juan Alvarez at Tombstone Cochise County Arizona Complaint filed warrant of arrest issued and delivered to Chief of Police James Coyle — No return. Recorders fees $1.25 not paid.

The Territory of Arizona
vs.
John Doe, Richard Roe, Bill Jones, Pat Smith, Richard Brady & Phill Earle, all persons whose true names are unknown.

Charge: Malicious Mischief Committed in Tombstone.

3rd. On this day Hop Lee made complaint on oath and in writing accusing the above named defendants of breaking the window and door window of his house shop and place of business — unlawfully & maliciously — Complaint filed and warrant issued and delivered to ____ no return. Recorders fees $1.25 not paid.

James Reilly
City Recorder

Court recordings

Historical Documents and Photographs of Tombstone

GRAND INVITATION BALL

GIVEN UNDER THE AUSPICES OF

COCHISE LODGE No. 5, I. O. O. F.,

Wednesday Evening, April 26th, 1882,

— AT —

SCHIEFFELIN HALL

Admit Mr. .... *and Ladies.*

TICKETS, ADMITTING GENTLEMAN AND LADIES, $3.00.

Not Transferable.

Prohibition:
Pouring out 500 gallons whiskey in Tombstone.

Historical Documents

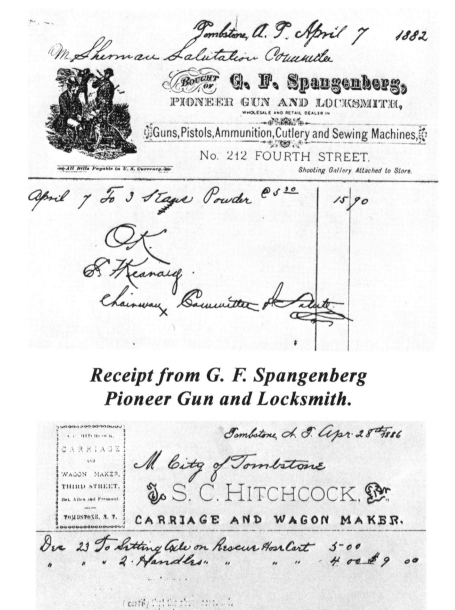

Receipt from G. F. Spangenberg
Pioneer Gun and Locksmith.

Repair receipt.

Historical Documents and Photographs of Tombstone

No.

IN THE RECORDER'S COURT, CITY OF TOMBSTONE,
CACHISE COUNTY, TERRITORY OF ARIZONA.

Before _____ Recorder.

The Mayor and Common Council of the City of Tombstone, Plaintiffs.

v.

Gee Wah and Charlie, (Chinamen) Defendant.

} Smoking opium {

Att'y for _____
Att'y for _____

188 6

DATE	PROCEEDINGS	PLAINTIFF'S COSTS
Jan 27	Defendants were charged by Chief Coyle with smoking opium. Defendants were brought before the court and plead not guilty. Upon trial they were convicted and fined $20. each and costs amounting to $24. or 34 days in jail. Charlie gave bond to pay fine, and Gee Wah was committed. Paid fine in February. *John Hume Recorder*	23 00

Mayor and Common Council
vs
Ah Chung

} Keeping opium joint {

| Jan 27 | Defendant was charged by Chief Coyle with keeping an opium joint. Defendant was brought into court and plead not guilty. Upon trial he was convicted and fined $50. and costs or 60 days in jail. Committed. *John Hume Recorder* | |

Gee Wah and Charlie (Chinamen) charged.

> Tombstone
> May 31st '09
>
> City of Tombstone
> Lum & Sing   №2
> To 64 meals @ $.30
> Per meal   19.20
>
> Ah Suen Ah Sing
>
> OK
> Geo. Bravin
> City Marshal

Ah Lum was China Mary's husband and Quong Kee's partner in the Can-Can.

Historical Documents and Photographs of Tombstone

The King of Tombstone's Chinatown in the 1880's.
—from a C.S. Fly Photo

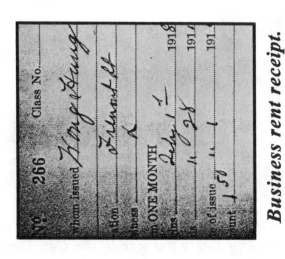

Business rent receipt.

A Colt single action pistol
once owned by Wyatt Earp. The pistol (serial number 69562) was made in 1881 and had been in the collection of Capt. Fred W. Dodge, Chief Special Officer for Wells Fargo & Co. Express.

WELLS FARGO SHOTGUN

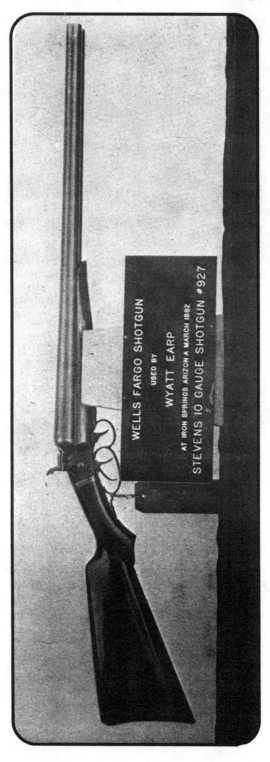

The shotgun which, it has been claimed, was used by Wyatt Earp to kill Curley Bill Brocius. Author James E. Earle purchased the shotgun in September of 1973 after making a special trip from Texas to Los Angeles where he made the bid for it during an auction. He calls it one of the last remaining links between two famous legends of the West - Tombstone and Wyatt Earp.

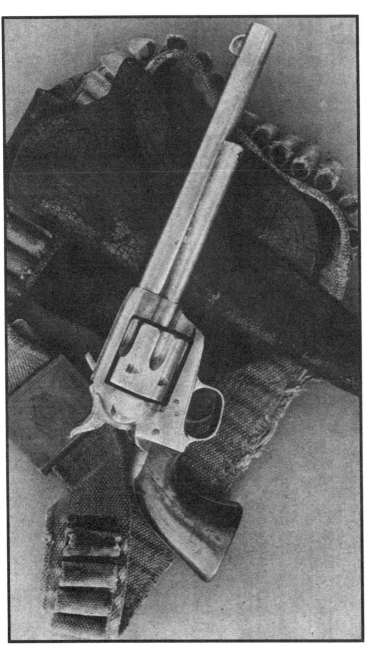

John P. Clum's Colt .44/40

As certified by John Davidson Vachon, the son of Caro Kingsland Clum Vachon, who was the daughter of Epitaph founder John P. Clum, this Colt .44/40 single action revolver with a 7 1/2-inch barrel (serial number 72157) was owned by the famed publisher until his death on May 2, 1932 in Los Angeles, Calif.

Here are the answers to the questions you wanted to know —

I was hunting Buffalo in the Winter of seventy three — and I went to Wichita in the spring of seventy three — If I told you the name of the man who both was hunting my arrest was Cod Pearce I told you wrong it was a mistake in my part, as his name was Shang Pearce — No Dr Holliday was not in El Paso while I was there — I donof remember anyone by the name of William Strahles in Tombstone — Pony Deal I was told went to new mexico with Johnny Barnes — Not one of the men you make mention of in your letter had notches in their guns. I have seen all of their guns, and know positively that none had notches

Wyatt Earp

A Letter from Wyatt Earp

TOMBSTONE EPITAPH   **NATIONAL EDITION**

TOMBSTONE CROWDED FOR GUNFIGHT ANNIVERSARY

THE WEATHERMAN had no sense for history, there were about 600 more witnesses and the action was recorded by dozens of cameras . . . but otherwise, the shootout which took place in Tombstone October 26 at the rear of the O.K. Corral followed the exact pattern of the fracas a hundred years earlier which made the town world-famous.

The Centennial of the O.K. Corral Gunfight was observed in balmy temperatures under a sunny sky, although the original event was fought on a blustery overcast day. A standing-room-only crowd of spectators from all over the country, Great Britain, France, Canada and Japan filled the site where the Earp brothers and Doc Holliday met the Clantons and McLaurys.

It was just about 2:30 p.m.—one hundred years later to the hour—when Tombstone's Wild Bunch, an organization of Western gunfight historians and actors, recreated the shootout which they have been portraying before audiences in Tombstone and throughout the country for many years.

The Wild Bunch, headed by Epitaph Associate Editor Ben Traywick, had alternated throughout the three-day Centennial observance period with another well-known group of Western gunfight historians, the Gallery of Gunfighters from Northern California, led by George Monte.

And adding still more color, action and excitement to the Corral scene throughout the long week-end were the Gunfighters of the Old West from Niles, California, and the Yankee Flat Raiders from Sacramento.

A feature at each show was the deft gun-handling and interesting and often amusing commentary of Phil Spangenberger, Associate Editor of *Guns & Ammo* magazine, and Editor of its Black Powder column.

Putting the large crowds each day in a frontier mood was an organization called the Real Old-Time Fiddlers from near-by Benson, which entertained before each performance.

EAGERLY AWAITED by the gun enthusiasts and collectors in the Sunday audience was the opening of a dozen sealed bids on an O.K. Corral Commemorative single-action Colt revolver. The historic weapon, manufactured in the same year as the Gunfight, had been completely restored under supervision of Colt authority John Kopec.

Phoenix insurance executive and gun collector Park Shaw bought the unique antique with a high bid of $11,000.

The restoration project was initiated by Harold O. Love, owner of the O.K. Corral, as the most appropriate way to commemorate the thirty seconds of American history.

However, Love's offer of $20,000 each for the weapons used by Frank McLaury and Billy Clanton in the O.K. Corral Gunfight, introduced as evidence at the murder charge preliminary hearing after the battle, failed to locate the guns.

THE NATION'S PRESS reported the Gunbattle of October 26, 1881 (see October *Epitaph*) and covered well and in detail the Centennial events. The Associated Press and United Press International sent reporters to Tombstone, as did the *New York Times*, *Philadelphia Inquirer*, the *Tucson Citizen*, *Arizona Star*, *Arizona Republic* and other papers. The historic event was the subject of documentaries on several Arizona television stations, and covered by the national television programs "Today" and "Good Morning, America."

And as it did 100 years ago, *The Tombstone Epitaph* is telling its readers what happened.

The Tombstone Epitaph, October 26, 1981

THE NEW YORK TIMES, MONDAY, OCTOBER 26, 1981

Town Built of Legends Keeps Wild West Alive

By WILLIAM K. STEVENS
Special to The New York Times

TOMBSTONE, Ariz., Oct. 25 — Around here, some folks still talk about Wyatt and Doc as if they were acquaintances you might meet any time at the big mahogany bar in the Crystal Palace Saloon. You can almost believe it — if you can ignore the Hondas, Kawasakis and Suzukis parked at the hitching rail nearby, and block out Reggie Jackson chasing a fly ball on the saloon's television set.

"I hear there's going to be a shooting down at the O.K. Corral," a sidewalk stroller said to his wife. And directly there was one. On one side, Wyatt, Morgan and Virgil Earp, menacing in their black greatcoats, black Stetsons, black vests and black string ties, advanced on Ike and Billy Clanton and Tom and Frank McLaury, cowboys all, on the other side.

There is a sudden flash and crash of gunfire at point-blank range. Now, as a century ago, it is all over in less than 30 seconds. Three men lie dead, two wounded, and the most infamous shoot-out in the history of the Old West is over. Burt Lancaster and Kirk Douglas, stars of perhaps the best-known movie version of the gunfight, would be proud.

At 28 seconds after 2:30 tomorrow afternoon, it will be exactly 100 years since the Gunfight at the O.K. Corral conferred mythic properties on what was then a scrubby but rich silver boom town full of every sort of opportunist and outlaw. The town is now a living museum piece a fraction of its size in the days of the Earps and the Clantons.

Throughout this weekend, the shoot-out was being re-enacted as authentically as possible by a local troupe of gunfighter-actors called The Wild Bunch. Tourists flocked to town to immerse themselves in a Western mystique that lives on here as perhaps nowhere else.

The New York Times/Oct. 26, 1981

Tombstone once was a thriving town of the old West

Tombstone in the 1880's had all the elements that Hollywood has long since transfigured into a uniquely American legend: Gunfighters, cowboys, rustlers, stage robbers, gamblers, Apaches, silver miners, vigilantes, lynchings, dance hall girls, big-name outlaws and lawmen alike. It was such a powerful mixture that even today, strained through a hundred years of dimming and distorting filters, it challenges even the most jaded imagination.

Maybe it is the Crystal Palace that does it, restored as it was 17 years ago to its 1881 look, with its huge mirrors behind the bar and its rows of tables along the opposite wall where Wyatt Earp and others ran faro and other card games.

Or maybe it is the Bird Cage Theater, with its original, wall-high, bullet-pockmarked painting of Fatima, later known as Little Egypt, and its 140 bullet holes in the walls and ceiling.

Or perhaps the stark landscape of Cochise County, rolling off in waves of mesquite to the distant mountains, where road signs read, "Caution: Open Range," and the cattle on the highway prove it.

14 Years as Wyatt Earp

Maybe, most of all, it is the frame of mind in which the keepers of the local legend approach their trust. Ben Traywick, the manager of a nearby explosives factory, has been portraying Wyatt Earp for 14 years, and plans to do so again in tomorrow's centennial shoot-out performance. "I've spent my whole life for this weekend," said the 54-year-old Mr. Traywick.

His son Bill, 24, a repair technician at an electronics plant outside Tucson, portrays 21-year-old Billy Clanton, one of the three men killed by the Earps and Doc Holliday. He has read much about Billy, and says, "I try to think like he thought." Doc Holliday and Morgan Earp, in Bill Traywick's eyes, were cold-blooded killers. "Doc," he says, "would have shot his own mother."

The argument over who were the good guys and who were the bad, which raged then, continues. The most commonly accepted version hereabouts is that the cowboys were not the trail drovers of the movies, but cutthroat rustlers and stage robbers. The Earps, who came to Tombstone from Dodge City, Kan., to make money just like everybody else, detested the cowboys as a threat to legitimate business, which in those days included gambling.

Bad blood simmered and finally boiled over in the confrontation at the O.K. Corral on Oct. 26, 1881. Actually, the shoot-out did not take place in the corral at all, contrary to the 1957 Lancaster-Douglas movie, but in a narrow lot between two buildings several feet away.

# About the Author

The first Traywick to arrive in America was John, who landed in Charleston, South Carolina in 1662. He had two sons, John and James, the former eventually settling in Tennessee and the latter in Alabama.

Ben T. Traywick, a descendent of John Traywick, was born in Watertown, Tennessee on August 3, 1927.

James Joseph Wiggins, Ben's maternal great-grandfather, was a private in the Confederate Army, Company B, 16th Tennessee Infantry Regiment. Private Wiggins was killed in Perryville, Kentucky on October 8, 1862.

Benjamin Abbot Traywick, Ben's paternal great-grandfather, was a First Sergeant in the Confederate Army, Company G, 28th Infantry (2nd Mountain Regiment Tennessee Volunteers). Sergeant Traywick participated in all of the battles waged across Tennessee and Mississippi, from Chattanooga to Shiloh. At the end of the war, he resumed farming on acreage owned by the family.

Like his predecessors, Ben T. Traywick was military minded and enlisted in the U.S. Navy during World War II although he was only 15 years old, being tall for his age. Assigned to the U.S.S. Jenkins DD447 (Fletcher Class Torpedo Destroyer), attached to the amphibious forces in the Pacific, he had earned ten Battle Stars and a Presidential Citation by his eighteenth birthday. He served a second hitch in the Navy in the late 1940s, most of it in China. When the Communists overran China, he was on the last ship to evacuate Tsingtao. The remainder of his enlistment was spent on the battleship Missouri.

Ben graduated from Tennessee Technological University with a B.S. Degree in Chemistry in 1953. After spending thirty years in exotic and high explosives in such places as Oak Ridge (Atomic); Sacramento (Missiles); and southeast Arizona (mining); he retired at the age of fifty-six.

Now he spends his time writing, researching Tombstone history, and visiting the far places in the American West and Mexico.

His first article was about a hillbilly sailor, called Saltwater McCoy. It was sold to "Our Navy" Magazine in 1957 and turned into a series. Ben has been frequently published in the Tombstone Epitaph since 1963. Since that beginning long ago, he has written more than six hundred newspaper and magazine articles. In addition, he has written forty-one pamphlets and books. His collection of "Earpiana" and Tombstone material is one of the best in existence anywhere.

Having been duly appointed by the Mayor and the City Council, Author Traywick is Tombstone's first and only City Historian to date. Ben and his wife, Red Marie, have lived in Tombstone since 1968. They have three children, Virginia Lynn, Mary Kate and William Maurice plus three Grandchildren; Benton Ivan, Rachel

Red Marie and Ben Traywick

Marie and Joshua Cody. They are co-founders of the "Wild Bunch" and "Hell's Belles," now famous after twenty-two years in the O.K. Corral and one hundred sixteen films as of 1993.

Together, Ben and Marie have created the Tombstone Book Series, a number of volumes that depict the local history as it actually was. It is their wish that you will find these volumes both interesting, entertaining and enlightening even as they have experienced in writing them.